GRAPHIC NONFICTION

HARRIET TUBMAN

THE LIFE OF AN
AFRICAN-AMERICAN ABOLITIONIST

by
ROB SHONE & ANITA GANERI

illustrated by
ROB SHONE

The Rosen Publishing Group, Inc., New York

Published in 2005 by The Rosen Publishing Group, Inc.
29 East 21st Street, New York, NY 10010

First edition, 2005

Designed and produced by
David West Books

Editor: Gail Bushnell
Photo Research: Carlotta Cooper

Photo credits:
Pages 5, 45 (both) – Rex Features Ltd.
Pages 6 (bottom), 7, 44 – Mary Evans Picture Library

Library of Congress Cataloging-in-Publication Data

Shone, Rob.
    Harriet Tubman : the life of an African-American abolitionist / by Rob Shone and
    Anita Ganeri.— 1st ed.
    p. cm. — (Graphic nonfiction)
    Includes index.
    ISBN 1-4042-0245-5 (lib. bdg.)
    1. Tubman, Harriet, 1820?–1913—Juvenile literature. 2. Slaves—United States—
    Biography—Juvenile literature. 3. African American women—Biography—Juvenile
    literature. 4. African American abolitionists—Biography—Juvenile literature. 5.
    African Americans—Biography—Juvenile literature. 6. Underground railroad—
    Juvenile literature. I. Ganeri, Anita, 1961– II. Title. III. Series.

    E444.T82S47 2005
    973.7'115'092—dc22

                                                          2004009649

Manufactured in China

CONTENTS

WHO'S WHO   3

THE UNDERGROUND RAILROAD   5

HARRIET TUBMAN'S WORLD   6

HARRIET TUBMAN:
THE LIFE OF AN AFRICAN-AMERICAN ABOLITIONIST 8

FREEDOM!   44

GLOSSARY   46

FOR MORE INFORMATION   47

INDEX and WEB SITES   48

WHO'S WHO

Harriet Tubman (c. 1822–1913) Born into slavery, Harriet escaped and helped free other slaves. During the American Civil War, she served as a soldier, a spy, and a nurse.

John Brown (1800–1858) Famous freedom fighter and abolitionist. Harriet met Brown in 1858. She helped him to gather slaves for a doomed rebellion.

Frederick Douglass (1818–1895) The son of a white father and a black slave mother. He escaped from slavery and became a leading abolitionist and antislavery campaigner.

Thomas Garrett (1789–1871) A Quaker and leading abolitionist from Delaware. His home was a station on the Underground Railroad for runaway slaves.

William Still (1821–1902) An escaped slave who became one of the leaders of the Underground Railroad. He kept records of the runaway slaves.

Susan B. Anthony (1820–1906) Active in the antislavery movement, she helped escaped slaves on the Underground Railroad. Leader of the campaign for women's suffrage.

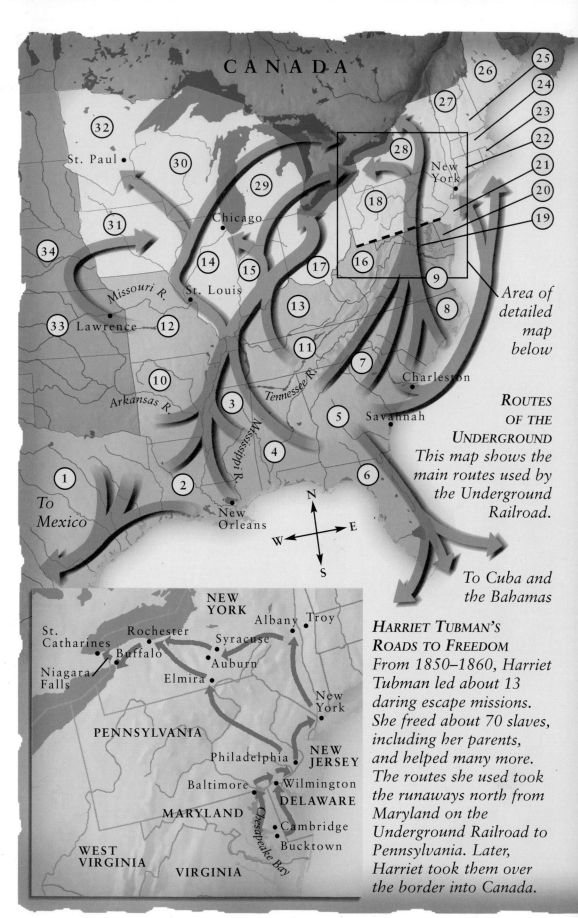

CANADA

32

St. Paul •

30

31

34

29

Chicago

14   15

St. Louis

33 Lawrence   12

Missouri R.

10

Arkansas R.

3

Tennessee R.

Mississippi R.

13

11

4

1

To
Mexico

2

New
Orleans

28

New
York

27   26

25
24
23
22
21
20
19

18

16

9

8

7

Charleston •

5

Savannah •

6

Area of
detailed
map
below

ROUTES
OF THE
UNDERGROUND
This map shows the
main routes used by
the Underground
Railroad.

N
W ←→ E
S

To Cuba and
the Bahamas

St.
Catharines

Niagara
Falls

Buffalo •

Rochester •

Syracuse •

Auburn •

Elmira •

Albany • Troy

New
York

NEW
YORK

PENNSYLVANIA

Philadelphia •

Baltimore •

MARYLAND

WEST
VIRGINIA

• Wilmington

NEW
JERSEY

DELAWARE

• Cambridge

• Bucktown

Chesapeake Bay

VIRGINIA

HARRIET TUBMAN'S
ROADS TO FREEDOM
From 1850–1860, Harriet
Tubman led about 13
daring escape missions.
She freed about 70 slaves,
including her parents,
and helped many more.
The routes she used took
the runaways north from
Maryland on the
Underground Railroad to
Pennsylvania. Later,
Harriet took them over
the border into Canada.

THE UNDERGROUND RAILROAD

Harriet Tubman was born into slavery in Maryland in about 1822. She managed to escape from her cruel masters. Harriet dedicated her life to fighting for freedom and justice. An active member of the Underground Railroad, she risked her life many times to help other runaway slaves.

FROM "EGYPT" TO "CANAAN"

The Bible tells how Moses led the Jews from slavery in Egypt to freedom in Canaan, the "Promised Land." For her work, Harriet was often called the "Moses" of her people.

KEY TO MAP

Free States   *Slave States*   *Territories*

Mason-Dixon Line – – – – – – – –
*The dividing line between
free and slave states.*

1 Texas 2 Louisiana 3 Mississippi
4 Alabama 5 Georgia 6 Florida
7 South Carolina 8 North Carolina
9 Virginia 10 Arkansas
11 Tennessee 12 Missouri
13 Kentucky 14 Illinois 15 Indiana
16 West Virginia 17 Ohio
18 Pennsylvania 19 Maryland
20 Delaware 21 New Jersey
22 Connecticut 23 Rhode Island
24 Massachusetts 25 New
Hampshire 26 Maine 27 Vermont
28 New York 29 Michigan
30 Wisconsin 31 Iowa
32 Minnesota 33 Kansas
34 Nebraska

$600 REWARD !

Left the service of the subscriber, near Port Republic, Calvert Co., Md.,

About the 19th of APRIL,

3 NEGRO SLAVES

REWARD POSTER

Anxious to get their slaves back, slave owners put up posters like the one above. Large rewards were offered for the capture and return of runaway slaves.

THE UNDERGROUND RAILROAD

The Underground Railroad was the network used by runaway slaves to escape from the slave states of the South to the free states of the North. Abolitionists' homes were "stations" where slaves received food, money, and shelter. The slaves were guided to safety by "conductors" who used covered wagons to carry slaves between stations, along routes called "rail tracks." By the middle of the nineteenth century, it was thought that some 50,000 slaves escaped using the railroad.

THE FUGITIVE SLAVE ACT

In 1850, the U.S. Congress passed the Fugitive Slave Act. It said that any marshall who did not arrest a runaway slave could be fined $1,000. Anyone helping a slave could be fined $1,000 and face six months in prison.

HARRIET TUBMAN'S WORLD

In Harriet Tubman's time, slavery was strong in the Southern states of the United States. In the North, however, antislavery campaigns were winning supporters.

A "PECULIAR INSTITUTION"
From the seventeenth century, black people were brought by force from Africa to work as slaves in North America. Chained together, the slaves were huddled on ships for the two-month voyage across the Atlantic Ocean. Conditions on board were terrible. As many as a third of the slaves died. On arrival, the slaves were sold at market to the highest bidder. Harriet Tubman's grandparents were probably captured as children in West Africa during the mid-1700s. The slave trade reached its peak in the eighteenth century, when millions of Africans were shipped over to America.

HARRIET TUBMAN
Harriet was the fifth of nine children of slaves Harriet Green and Benjamin Ross.

WORKING IN THE FIELDS
Tens of thousands of slaves were bought by Southern plantation owners to work in the cotton fields.

KING COTTON
The slaves were put to work on vast plantations owned by white planters. Slaves had a hard life, with heavy work and long hours. Most lived in poor conditions and were badly treated, underfed, and whipped or beaten. Many died soon after they reached the plantations. In the South, cotton was the backbone of the economy. Picking cotton took a great deal of work and required large numbers of slaves.

Confederate States — *1 Texas 2 Louisiana 3 Mississippi 4 Alabama 5 Georgia 6 Florida 7 South Carolina 8 North Carolina 9 Virginia 10 Arkansas 11 Tennessee*

Union States — *12 Missouri 13 Kentucky 14 Illinois 15 Indiana 16 West Virginia 17 Ohio 18 Pennsylvania 19 Maryland 20 Delaware 21 New Jersey 22 Connecticut 23 Rhode Island 24 Massachusetts 25 New Hampshire 26 Maine 27 Vermont 28 New York 29 Michigan 30 Wisconsin 31 Iowa 32 Minnesota*

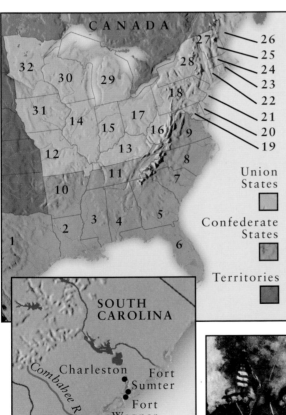

THE AMERICAN CIVIL WAR

By the early nineteenth century, the Northern and Southern states of the United States had many social and economic differences. Slavery was abolished in the North in 1820. The cotton plantations of the South relied on a huge slave labor force. The plantation owners wanted to keep slavery in place. In 1861, 11 Southern states broke away from the Union to form their own confederacy. Confederate troops attacked the Union garrison at Fort Sumter, South Carolina. This began the American Civil War. Four years of bitter fighting followed. Finally, in April 1865, the Confederate army surrendered and the Union claimed victory.

THE BATTLE OF GETTYSBURG

Gettysburg (below) was one of the most important battles of the Civil War. It was fought in July 1863 in Gettysburg, Pennsylvania. The Union won the battle.

HARRIET TUBMAN'S WAR

Tubman spent most of the American Civil War in the Port Royal area of South Carolina.

HARRIET TUBMAN

THE LIFE OF AN AFRICAN-AMERICAN ABOLITIONIST

IT IS 1745. OFF THE COAST OF AFRICA, A TRADING SHIP HEADS HOME TO AMERICA...

...WITH A HOLD FULL OF SLAVES.

SHARING IN THE SUFFERING AND MISERY OF THEIR FELLOW CAPTIVES ARE THE FUTURE GRANDPARENTS OF HARRIET TUBMAN.

AUBURN, NEW YORK, 1896. A THUNDERSTORM BREAKS, DRENCHING THE TOWN.

MAMA MOSES! HARRIET! IT'S RAINING HARD!

IS IT NOW?

YOU'D BETTER COME IN. GO SIT BY THE FIRE AND GET DRY.

AND I EXPECT YOU'LL BE WANTING SOME CANDY. GOOD THING I KEEP SOME FOR **SPECIAL** GUESTS.

MAMA MOSES, TELL US ABOUT WHEN YOU WERE A SLAVE AND FREED ALL THOSE OTHER SLAVES.

AGAIN?

YES!

YES!

WELL, MY GRANDPARENTS CAME FROM AFRICA. THEY WERE CAPTURED AND SOLD TO THE SLAVERS...

HARRIET'S GRANDPARENTS WERE BROUGHT TO AMERICA AND SOLD AS IF THEY WERE PROPERTY, LIKE SHEEP OR HORSES.

HER PARENTS, BEN ROSS AND HARRIET GREEN, WERE BORN SLAVES IN DORCHESTER COUNTY, MARYLAND. THEY WERE OWNED BY DIFFERENT MASTERS, BUT THEY GOT MARRIED IN ABOUT 1808. THEY LIVED NEAR THE BLACKWATER RIVER.

HARRIET WAS BORN IN ABOUT 1822 AND NAMED ARAMINTA, OR MINTY FOR SHORT. SHE WAS THE FIFTH OF NINE CHILDREN. HER FATHER MANAGED A TIMBER BUSINESS FOR HIS MASTER.

FOR A TIME SHE WAS HAPPY. THEN, IN 1824, HER MOTHER'S OWNER, EDWARD BRODESS, MOVED TEN MILES AWAY. HE TOOK HARRIET'S MOTHER AND THE CHILDREN WITH HIM, LEAVING HER FATHER BEHIND.

HARRIET WAS ABOUT FIVE WHEN SHE WAS TAKEN AWAY FROM HER FAMILY...

SHE'LL MAKE A **FINE WORKER.** YOU JUST GIVE HER BOARD AND LODGINGS.

SHE WAS *YOUNG, SCARED,* AND **HOMESICK.**

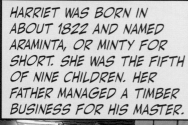

HARRIET'S NEW MASTERS TRIED TO TEACH HER WEAVING. WHEN THAT DIDN'T WORK, THEY MADE HER CHECK THE MUSKRAT TRAPS. SHE GOT MEASLES AND ALMOST *DIED.*

THEN HARRIET'S MASTERS MADE HER DO HOUSEKEEPING CHORES, BUT NO ONE SHOWED HER WHAT TO DO. THE MISTRESS THOUGHT A **BEATING** WAS THE CURE FOR HER IGNORANCE.

HARRIET JUST WASN'T SUITED TO DOING INDOOR WORK.

TCHANKK!

HER BEST WAS NEVER GOOD ENOUGH.

ONE OF HER CHORES WAS AS A NURSEMAID.

SHE HAD TO STOP THE BABY FROM WAKING UP THE MISTRESS.

IT WASN'T ALWAYS EASY TO STAY AWAKE ALL NIGHT.

OFTEN, SHE WOULD FINALLY GET TO BED NURSING HER *BRUISES* INSTEAD OF A BABY.

HHHAAAAAAA!!!

12

WHEN HARRIET WAS ABOUT 13, SHE WAS SENT ON AN ERRAND TO THE LOCAL STORE. A SLAVE HAD GONE INTO THE STORE WITHOUT HIS OWNER'S APPROVAL.

THE SLAVE'S OVERSEER HAD FOLLOWED HIM AND THREATENED TO BEAT HIM. NATURALLY, THE SLAVE RAN AWAY. THE OVERSEER PICKED UP AN IRON WEIGHT AND THREW IT AT THE SLAVE.

SOMEHOW IT HIT HARRIET.

YOU ALRIGHT?

MINTY? MINTY?

HARRIET'S HEAD WAS BADLY INJURED. SHE BEGAN TO HAVE **STRANGE DREAMS**...

IN ONE, HARRIET WAS FLYING OVER FIELDS. SOME BEAUTIFUL WHITE WOMEN WERE HOLDING THEIR ARMS OUT TO HER, BUT SHE COULDN'T REACH THEM. HARRIET'S HEAD SLOWLY GOT BETTER, BUT SHE STARTED HAVING **SLEEPING SPELLS**. HARRIET WOULD FALL ASLEEP ANYWHERE, ANYTIME.

13

IN 1836, HARRIET WAS HIRED OUT TO JOHN STEWART, A WOOD MERCHANT AND SHIPBUILDER.

SHE COULD DO THE WORK JUST AS WELL AS THE MEN.

WORKING IN THE WOODS MEANT SHE COULD SEE HER FATHER MORE OFTEN.

WHO ARE THOSE MEN, PA?

FREEMEN FROM BALTIMORE. THEY'RE HERE BUYING TIMBER.

HARRIET DIDN'T OFTEN GET THE CHANCE TO HEAR NEWS FROM OUTSIDE THE COUNTY...

WE HEARD SLAVES ARE BEING HELPED TO ESCAPE NORTH.

A GANG OF ABOLITIONISTS IS WORKING IN SECRET TO SET SLAVES FREE.

THE NEWS GAVE HER HOPE.

HARRIET SAVED MONEY AND BOUGHT A PAIR OF STEERS. IT MEANT SHE COULD HIRE HERSELF OUT IN HER SPARE TIME.

HARRIET WAS NOW 22. HER MOTHER HAD PLANS FOR HER...

MARRIAGE? WHO WOULD WANT TO MARRY ME? BECAUSE OF MY ILLNESS, I'M NOT THOUGHT MUCH OF AS A SLAVE LET ALONE AS A WIFE!

SHE WAS WRONG, THOUGH. SOMEONE WAS INTERESTED.

JOHN TUBMAN WAS HIS NAME. HE WAS A FREEMAN, WORKING ON THE LOCAL FARMS. IT WASN'T USUAL FOR A SLAVE TO MARRY A FREEMAN BUT HARRIET'S MASTER AGREED. SHE CHANGED HER SLAVE NAME, ARAMINTA, TO HARRIET AT THIS TIME.

THEN IN 1849, HARRIET'S MASTER, EDWARD BRODESS, DIED.

HARRIET HAD BEEN TOLD THAT SHE WOULD NEVER BE SOLD INTO THE SOUTH. BUT BRODESS'S WIDOW WAS LEFT WITH DEBTS.

THE SOUTH WAS IN NEED OF SLAVES. MANY TIMES, HARRIET HAD SEEN LONG LINES OF POOR PEOPLE CHAINED AND ROPED TOGETHER LIKE ANIMALS. HARRIET LEARNED THAT SHE AND HER BROTHERS WERE GOING TO THE SOUTH.

FOR SOME PEOPLE, GOING SOUTH WAS LIKE A DEATH SENTENCE!

IN EARLY OCTOBER, HARRIET DECIDED TO ESCAPE NORTH. SHE WANTED TO TAKE JOHN WITH HER BUT HE WOULDN'T GO. SHE JUST WALKED THROUGH THE GATE AND KEPT ON GOING.

A NEIGHBOR GAVE HARRIET THE NAMES OF ABOLITIONISTS WHO WOULD SHELTER HER ON THE WAY.

HARRIET DIDN'T KNOW THE WAY BUT SHE HAD A GUIDE. IT WAS 'THE DRINKING GOURD,' A GROUP OF STARS WITH THE NORTH STAR AT ITS TAIL. SHE FOLLOWED THAT STAR, KNOWING IT WOULD LEAD HER NORTH, TO FREEDOM AND THE 'PROMISED LAND.'

AFTER DAYS OF TRAVELING, SHE CROSSED THE MASON-DIXON LINE INTO THE FREE STATE OF PENNSYLVANIA.

HARRIET LOOKED AT HER HANDS TO SEE IF SHE WAS THE SAME PERSON. IT FELT LIKE SHE HAD REACHED HEAVEN!

HARRIET ARRIVED IN PHILADELPHIA AND FOUND HERSELF IN A **STRANGE LAND.**

SHE WAS FREE BUT HER FAMILY AND FRIENDS WERE STILL SLAVES. SHE DECIDED THEY SHOULD BE **FREE,** TOO!

SHE GOT WORK AND SAVED EVERY PENNY SHE COULD.

THEN A FRIEND BROUGHT HER BAD NEWS.

HARRIET, YOUR NIECE KESSIAH AND HER TWO CHILDREN — THEY'RE GOING TO BE **SOLD!**

HARRIET USED THE MONEY SHE HAD SAVED TO GO TO BALTIMORE. THEN SHE AND JOHN BOWLEY, KESSIAH'S HUSBAND, MADE PLANS. IT WASN'T SAFE FOR HER TO GO FARTHER, SO JOHN WENT TO DORCHESTER COUNTY ALONE.

THE SALE WAS HELD AT CAMBRIDGE...

SOLD!

KLAKK!

AFTER THE SALE...

NOW WHERE'S THAT BUYER?

GONE? SOMEONE'S PLAYED A **JOKE** ON US.

BRING THE WOMAN BACK. WE'LL START THE SALE AGAIN.

WHAT WOMAN? THERE'S NO WOMAN HERE!

THE BUYER HADN'T COME FORWARD BECAUSE IT WAS JOHN BOWLEY HIMSELF! AND AT THAT VERY MOMENT, JOHN WAS LEADING KESSIAH AND THEIR TWO CHILDREN TO SAFETY AT A FRIEND'S HOUSE.

THAT EVENING, JOHN BOWLEY AND HIS FAMILY SET OFF ON THE **DANGEROUS** JOURNEY UP CHESAPEAKE BAY TO BALTIMORE.

A FEW MONTHS LATER, HARRIET RETURNED TO BALTIMORE AND HELPED THREE OTHER SLAVES ESCAPE. IN 1851, SHE FELT SAFE ENOUGH TO GO BACK TO DORCHESTER COUNTY.

SHE WANTED TO BRING HER HUSBAND, JOHN, BACK WITH HER. BUT HE DIDN'T WANT TO GO. HE HAD GOTTEN MARRIED AGAIN! HARRIET'S DREAM OF LIVING FREE WITH HER HUSBAND WAS OVER.

HARRIET MADE MOST OF HER TRIPS ON LONG WINTER NIGHTS. SHE WOULD MEET HER GROUP AWAY FROM THE PLANTATIONS. GRAVEYARDS WERE GOOD SPOTS.

WHEN IT WAS CLEAR, HARRIET WOULD SING A SPIRITUAL. THE SONGS HAD HIDDEN MEANING FOR THE SLAVES. SATURDAY NIGHT WAS A GOOD TIME TO LEAVE. REWARD POSTERS WOULDN'T GET PUT UP UNTIL MONDAY.

THEY TRAVELED BY NIGHT...

...AND HID DURING THE DAY – IN ANY PLACE THEY COULD FIND.

SOMETIMES THEY HID UNDER THE NOSES OF THE PEOPLE TRYING TO CATCH THEM!

HARRIET USED DISGUISES...

...AND OTHER TRICKS. SHE WOULD BUY CHICKENS AND LET THEM LOOSE IF SHE MET AN OLD MASTER.

COME BACK HERE, YOU RASCALS!

THE SLAVE OWNERS DIDN'T KNOW IT WAS HARRIET HELPING FREE THEIR SLAVES. BUT THE ABOLITIONISTS IN THE NORTH AND THE LEADERS OF THE **UNDERGROUND RAILROAD** DID.

THIS RAILROAD DIDN'T HAVE REAL TRAINS, TRACKS, OR STATIONS. THE **TRAINS** WERE THE GROUPS OF FLEEING SLAVES. THE **TRACKS** WERE THE SECRET ESCAPE ROUTES NORTH. THE **STATIONS** WERE THE HOUSES ALONG THE WAY WHERE THE SLAVES COULD FIND SAFETY.

THE STATIONS WERE RUN BY **STATIONMASTERS** WHO LOOKED AFTER THEIR PART OF THE TRACK AND HID THE RUNAWAYS. THE SLAVES WERE CALLED **PASSENGERS** OR **FREIGHT**. THE **CONDUCTOR** GUIDED THEM TO FREEDOM.

IN 1854, HARRIET WENT TO THE UNDERGROUND'S NEW YORK OFFICES. SHE MET WILLIAM STILL, ONE OF ITS LEADERS, AND BECAME A CONDUCTOR.

MY JOB IS TO WRITE DOWN THE NAMES OF THE RUNAWAYS AND WHERE THEY'RE FROM. THAT WAY THEY MIGHT MEET UP WITH THEIR FAMILIES AGAIN, ONE DAY.

BY NOW, THE LAW HAD BEEN CHANGED.* RUNAWAYS WEREN'T SAFE, EVEN IN FREE STATES. HARRIET HAD TO MOVE HER PEOPLE TO **CANADA**, WHERE THE AMERICAN LAWS DID NOT APPLY.

THEY WENT TO ST. CATHARINES, JUST NORTH OF THE BORDER. THEIR FIRST WINTER WAS COLD AND HARD.

*THE FUGITIVE SLAVE ACT, SEE PAGE 5.

IN 1857, HARRIET HAD HEARD THAT HER FATHER WAS GOING TO BE ARRESTED FOR HELPING RUNAWAYS. SHE WANTED TO BRING HER PARENTS NORTH TO SAFETY.

SHE BUILT A BUGGY FROM BITS AND PIECES AND BOUGHT A HORSE. THEY DIDN'T RIDE IN STYLE, BUT HER PLAN WORKED.

BACK IN HARRIET'S HOME, 1896...

HOW MANY TRIPS SOUTH DID YOU MAKE, MAMA MOSES?

ELEVEN OR 12, MAYBE 13. I BROUGHT AS MANY AS 70 OR 80 PEOPLE TO THE 'PROMISED LAND.' I ALSO HELPED 50 OR 60 MORE BY TELLING THEM WHICH WAY TO GO.

I NEVER THOUGHT OF MY OWN SAFETY, JUST MY 'FREIGHT.'

BY AROUND 1859, IT GOT TOO RISKY FOR ME TO KEEP GOING TO MARYLAND. I HAD A PRICE ON MY HEAD.

WELL, IF I WERE TO DESCRIBE A JOURNEY USING BITS FROM A FEW OF THEM, I SUPPOSE IT MIGHT GO LIKE THIS...

WHAT WOULD A TRIP BE LIKE FROM BEGINNING TO END?

HARRIET BEGINS HER STORY...

A TRIP WOULD START ON A SATURDAY NIGHT IN WINTERTIME. I'D START SINGING...

STEAL AWAY, STEAL AWAY, STEAL AWAY TO JESUS.

DORCHESTER COUNTY, MARYLAND, 1856...

THE SIGN! FIRST ONE, THEN TWO... FINALLY, HALF A DOZEN SCARED FIGURES *CREPT* OUT OF THE *SHADOWS.*

STEAL AWAY, STEAL AWAY HOME. I AIN'T GOT LONG TO STAY HERE.

HARRIET PUT HER PLAN INTO ACTION.

COME ON!

THINGS DID NOT GO SMOOTHLY. AT A STATION...

...THE STATIONMASTER NO LONGER LIVED THERE.

WHO'S THERE? RUNAWAY SLAVES!

HUNTED, THEY WERE FORCED TO HIDE...

SOME OF THE 'FREIGHT' HAD SECOND THOUGHTS...

THEY'RE GOING TO *CATCH* US FOR SURE. IF WE GO BACK NOW, MAYBE THEY WON'T NOTICE WE'VE GONE.

I'M STAYING HERE. I'M SO TIRED, I COULD SLEEP FOR A WEEK.

LET ME *STOP* YOU RIGHT THERE!

NO ONE'S GOING BACK.

YOU'D BE PUTTING THE WHOLE UNDERGROUND IN **DANGER**. AND WE CAN'T STAY HERE. THEY'LL SOON FIGURE OUT WHERE WE ARE. YOU HAVE **NO CHOICE**.

MOVE...

...OR DIE!

K-KLACKK!

SSSH...QUIET!

A MAN APPROACHED. HE SEEMED TO BE TALKING TO HIMSELF!

IF SOME FOLK WERE TO GO DOWN THE LANE, THEY MAY FIND A FARM. IN THE BARN, THEY MAY FIND A HORSE AND CART.

IF SOME FOLK WERE TO BORROW THAT CART, MAYBE THEY COULD LEAVE IT WITH A GOOD QUAKER FAMILY SO THAT IT CAN BE RETURNED.

THEY TOOK HIS ADVICE, FOUND THE CART, AND MOVED ON.

THEY HAD GOOD REASON TO KEEP MOVING – *SLAVE CATCHERS*.

I WANT THEM BACK, BRET, UNHARMED!

WHILE HER PASSENGERS HID, HARRIET MADE A DANGEROUS TRIP TO BUY FOOD IN A NEARBY TOWN. SHE WORE A SUNBONNET TO HIDE HER FACE.

LOOK HERE! $10,000 REWARD FOR THE CAPTURE, DEAD OR ALIVE, OF ONE HARRIET TUBMAN, RUNAWAY SLAVE. SHE IS DARK SKINNED, SMALL IN HEIGHT, AND ILLITERATE.

HARRIET TURNED A CORNER AND WALKED STRAIGHT INTO A FORMER MASTER!

WATCH WHERE YOU'RE GOING!

HMM, CAN IT BE?

HARRIET HAD TO THINK QUICKLY.

FORTUNATELY, HARRIET HELD THE NEWSPAPER THE RIGHT WAY UP!

NO, IT'S NOT HARRIET. SHE CAN'T READ!

HARRIET DID ONE LAST THING BEFORE LEAVING TOWN.

HARRIET AND HER PASSENGERS REACHED WILMINGTON. THEY HAD TO GET TO THE STATION, BUT ALL THE ROADS INTO TOWN WERE BEING WATCHED. SLAVE CATCHERS WERE ON THE LOOKOUT FOR THEM.

A WAGON CARRYING BRICKLAYERS DROVE PAST THE BARRICADE OF SLAVE CATCHERS...

IT STOPPED VERY CLOSE TO WHERE HARRIET WAS HIDING.

HARRIET, HARRIET TUBMAN. MOSES, ARE YOU THERE? THOMAS GARRETT SENT ME TO TAKE YOU TO THE STATION.

LATER, THE CART RETURNED THE WAY IT CAME, PAST THE BARRICADE. THIS TIME IT WAS CARRYING MORE THAN JUST A LOAD OF BRICKS.

IT'S SAFE. YOU CAN COME OUT NOW.

SHORTLY...

THOMAS GARRETT!

HARRIET! I AM GLAD THOU ART SAFE. I WILL HAVE FOOD BROUGHT FOR THEE.

I WILL ALSO GIVE THEE MONEY TO BUY NEW SHOES.

HE TALKS FUNNY! IS HE A REVEREND, HARRIET?

HE'S A QUAKER. THEY TALK THE WAY THE BIBLE IS WRITTEN. THEY'RE GOOD PEOPLE. I TRUST THEM AS MUCH AS I TRUST MY OWN.

HARRIET AND HER GROUP TRAVELED THROUGH THE NIGHT. IT WAS NEARLY MORNING AND THEY WERE EAGER TO REACH THE NEXT STATION, AND SAFETY.

WE HAVE TO KEEP MOVING. WE DON'T WANT TO BE CAUGHT IN THE OPEN WHEN IT'S LIGHT.

SUDDENLY, HARRIET SENSED DANGER...

?!!

DOGS!

TIRED AS THEY WERE, THE RUNAWAYS HEADED FOR THE TREES, AS FAST AS THEY COULD.

QUICK! EVERYBODY HEAD FOR THOSE TREES. THERE'S A RIVER THROUGH THE WOODS. MAYBE WE CAN THROW THEM OFF OUR SCENT.

STOP!

THE RIVER WAS FROZEN. IF THEY CROSSED THE ICE, THE DOGS WOULD PICK UP THEIR SCENT!

HARRIET HAD AN IDEA...

EVERYBODY! GET ON THE ICE. GO THAT WAY.

DOWN THE RIVER, THE ICE HAD BROKEN UP.

GET IN THE WATER! MAKE FOR THAT BARE PATCH BUT KEEP OFF THE SNOW. THEN HIDE!

DUNFFF!

LOOK! THE SNOW HAS BEEN DISTURBED AND THE ICE BROKEN. THEY'RE ON THE OTHER BANK!

IT WON'T FOOL THEM FOR LONG. KEEP UP. THE STATION IS NOT FAR.

FINALLY, AT FREDERICK DOUGLASS'S STATION...

HARRIET, THERE ARE SLAVERS EVERYWHERE LOOKING FOR YOU. FOLLOW ME.

DOWN HERE! STAY QUIET! I'LL TELL YOU WHEN IT'S SAFE.

OH, NO! NOT NOW! HUSH, HONEY, HUSH.

WHIMPER WHIMPER

HERE, LET ME.

IT'S A SEDATIVE. ANYONE ELSE FEELING NERVOUS?

ZZZZZ

HARRIET TOOK OUT A SMALL BOTTLE FROM HER BAG.

HARRIET AND HER PASSENGERS TRAVELED STEADILY NORTH. AT LONG LAST, THEY STOOD OUTSIDE THE RAILWAY STATION AT BUFFALO, A SHORT RIDE AWAY FROM FREEDOM. THEN HARRIET SAW THEM...

SLAVE CATCHERS!

QUICK! WE GOT TO GET A TRAIN HEADING THE OTHER WAY.

THEY WON'T THINK TO LOOK FOR RUNAWAYS GOING SOUTH!

THEY CHANGED TRAINS AT THE NEXT STATION. BEFORE LONG, THEY PASSED OVER THE NIAGARA FALLS, THE GATEWAY TO CANADA.

THEY TOOK IN THE SIGHT OF THE FALLS. ONLY JOE BAILEY DID NOT LOOK. THE CLOSER THEY GOT TO FREEDOM, THE MORE HE FEARED CAPTURE.

COME AND LOOK AT THE FALLS, JOE.

AT LAST, THEIR ORDEAL WAS OVER.

NEXT JOURNEY I TAKE, IT'LL BE TO HEAVEN!

MIGHT'VE LOOKED AT THE FALLS FIRST, JOE!

HARRIET HAS FINISHED HER STORY...

NOW, ALL THOSE THINGS DIDN'T HAPPEN ON ONE TRIP. BUT THEY ALL HAPPENED – AND PLENTY MORE.

NOT ALL THE SLAVES I HELPED FREE WERE PLANNED ESCAPES, THOUGH. ON ONE OCCASION, IN 1860, I WAS GOING TO ALBANY AND HAD TO PASS THROUGH TROY, IN NEW YORK STATE.

A RUNAWAY SLAVE CALLED CHARLES NALLE WAS BEING HELD IN THE MARSHALL'S OFFICE.

HIS MASTER WANTED HIM BACK. A CROWD OF A THOUSAND WERE WAITING TO CATCH A SIGHT OF CHARLES.

EVENTUALLY, THE POLICE BROUGHT HIM OUT. HIS HANDS WERE CHAINED.

HE WAS ONE-EIGHTH COLORED AND AS WHITE AS THE OFFICERS HOLDING HIM.

I RUSHED FORWARD AND GRABBED CHARLES. I WASN'T GOING TO LET HIM GO UNTIL HE WAS FREE.

THEN IT SEEMED LIKE A FULL-SCALE **BATTLE** BEGAN – WITH ME IN THE MIDDLE.

THE POLICE OFFICERS WERE RAINING DOWN **BLOWS** ON ME WITH THEIR STICKS. BUT I **HUNG** ON IN.

WE BROKE FREE AND REACHED THE RIVER FERRY. BUT CHARLES WAS CAUGHT AGAIN ON THE OTHER SIDE AND TAKEN INTO A HOUSE.

THE MOB STORMED HIS NEW PRISON AND HIS CAPTORS OPENED FIRE. MORE THAN ONE MAN FELL **DEAD**.

THE REST OF US PULLED CHARLES FREE. OUTSIDE, WE BROKE OFF THE CHAINS FROM HIS BLEEDING HANDS AND THREW THEM IN THE RIVER. THEN HE MADE HIS ESCAPE. LATER ON, THE PEOPLE OF TROY HELPED BUY HIS FREEDOM.

BDOUSHH!

YOU'RE A GOOD STORYTELLER, MAMA.

I'VE HAD LOTS OF PRACTICE, TELLING MY TALES TO ABOLITIONISTS.

I MET SOME GOOD PEOPLE LIKE LUCRETIA AND MARTHA COFFIN MOTT, SOJOURNER TRUTH, WENDELL PHILLIPS, AND GERRIT SMITH.

THE ABOLITIONISTS FOUGHT FOR THE CAUSE OF FREEDOM. CAPTAIN JOHN BROWN WAS A ABOLITIONIST.

BROWN HAD BEEN FIGHTING THE SLAVERS IN KANSAS AND HAD GONE NORTH TO GET SUPPORT. HE HAD HEARD OF HARRIET FROM FREDERICK DOUGLASS. IN 1858, HE VISITED HER IN ST. CATHARINES.

GENERAL TUBMAN! GENERAL TUBMAN! GENERAL TUBMAN!

BROWN WANTED TO START A SLAVE UPRISING IN THE SOUTH. HE ASKED HARRIET TO GATHER SLAVES, SCOUT THE AREA, AND HELP WITH PLANS FOR THE RAID.

ON OCTOBER 16, 1859, BROWN AND 21 OTHERS RODE INTO HARPERS FERRY, WEST VIRGINIA, TO CAPTURE THE WEAPONS STORE. HE WANTED GUNS TO ARM THE SLAVES THAT HE HOPED WOULD JOIN HIM.

BUT THE SLAVES DIDN'T FOLLOW. TWO DAYS LATER, THE UPRISING WAS HALTED. BROWN WAS CAPTURED AND TEN LAY DEAD, INCLUDING HIS TWO SONS. BROWN WAS TRIED FOR TREASON AND HUNG. HARRIET KNEW WAR WAS COMING, AND WITH IT FREEDOM.

IN APRIL 1861, CONFEDERATE GUNS OPENED FIRE ON FORT SUMTER IN SOUTH CAROLINA. JOHN ANDREWS, THE GOVERNOR OF MASSACHUSETTS, THOUGHT HARRIET WOULD BE USEFUL TO THE UNION. IN JANUARY 1862, SHE WENT TO THE PORT ROYAL AREA OF SOUTH CAROLINA.

HARRIET THOUGHT SHE WAS GOING AS A SCOUT. SHE WAS WRONG.

THE ARMY CALLS THEM **CONTRABAND** – THE SLAVES FREED BY THE FIGHTING. THEY DON'T KNOW HOW TO CARE FOR THEMSELVES. SEE WHAT YOU CAN DO FOR THEM.

HARRIET SET UP A LAUNDRY SO THAT THE WOMEN COULD EARN MONEY CLEANING THE SOLDIERS' CLOTHES.

TO EARN MONEY FOR HERSELF, HARRIET MADE PIES AND ROOT BEER TO SELL TO THE TROOPS.

HARRIET HELPED IN OTHER WAYS, TOO.

IT'S HARD TO STOP DISEASE, HARRIET. CONDITIONS ARE SO BAD.

SHE CURED FEVERS, USING MEDICINES MADE FROM PLANTS AND ROOTS.

AS WELL AS THE SICK, THE NURSES HAD TO TREAT THE WOUNDED...

...SOMETIMES ON THE BATTLEFIELD — WITH BULLETS FLYING AROUND THEIR HEADS.

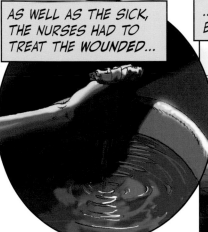

IN THE SPRING OF 1862, GENERAL HUNTER ARRIVED AT PORT ROYAL. HE SET UP THE FIRST UNOFFICIAL REGIMENT OF BLACK SOLDIERS. THEY LATER BECAME THE OFFICIAL FIRST SOUTH CAROLINA VOLUNTEERS.

ON JANUARY 1, 1863, THE UNION DECLARED THAT ALL SLAVES WERE *FREE!* HARRIET AND HER FRIENDS HELD A CELEBRATION IN THE WOODS.

MEANWHILE, HUNTER SAW THAT HARRIET COULD BE USEFUL AS A SCOUT AND SPY. SHE ORGANIZED SOME CONTRABANDS TO HELP. THEY WENT INLAND, GATHERING ALL THE INFORMATION THEY COULD.

IT WAS EASY FOR HARRIET TO FIND HER WAY AROUND. THE LAND WAS LIKE HER HOME, WITH RIVERS AND CREEKS SNAKING THROUGH MARSHES.

HARRIET'S GROUP WOULD SNEAK ACROSS CONFEDERATE LINES...

...AND GET INFORMATION FROM THE LOCAL SLAVES.

THEY REPORTED TO GENERALS HUNTER, STEVENS, AND SHERMAN.

IN JUNE 1863, GENERAL HUNTER ASKED HARRIET TO SCOUT THE COMBAHEE RIVER PLANTATIONS. THE UNION WANTED TO DESTROY THE ENEMY SUPPLIES THERE. SHE HELPED PLAN THE RAID WITH COLONEL JAMES MONTGOMERY, A FRIEND OF JOHN BROWN.

HARRIET WAS TO LEAD 300 MEN FROM THE SECOND SOUTH CAROLINA VOLUNTEERS.

THE RAID BEGAN ON JUNE 2. FIRST, THE RIVER WAS CLEARED OF CONFEDERATE MINES...

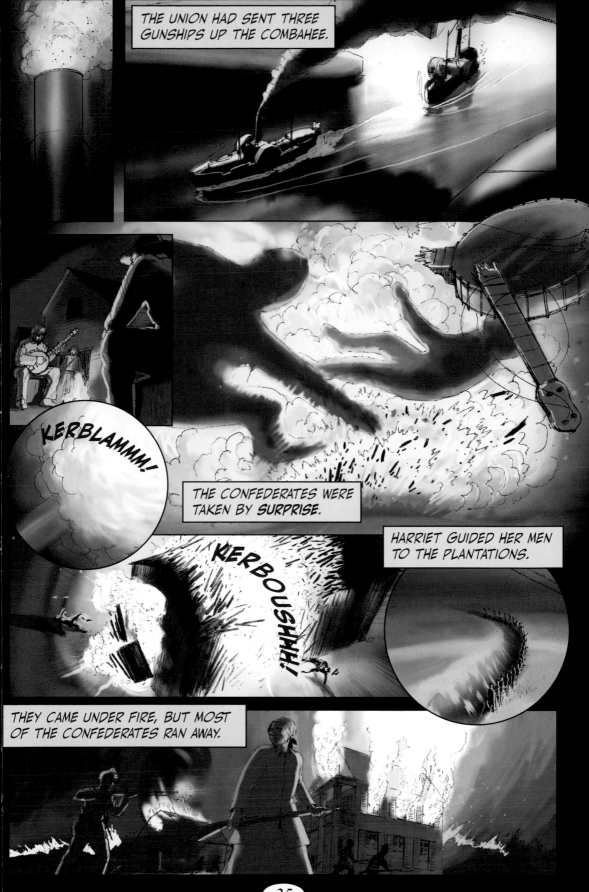

THE UNION HAD SENT THREE GUNSHIPS UP THE COMBAHEE.

KERBLAMMM!

THE CONFEDERATES WERE TAKEN BY SURPRISE.

HARRIET GUIDED HER MEN TO THE PLANTATIONS.

KERBOUSHH!

THEY CAME UNDER FIRE, BUT MOST OF THE CONFEDERATES RAN AWAY.

THE SLAVES WERE JUST AS SCARED OF THE 'YANKEE BUCKRA' AS THEY WERE OF THEIR OWN MASTERS. BUT THEY SOON GOT OVER THEIR FEAR AND THE DRIVERS' WHIPS – AND TRIED TO ESCAPE.

THEY TOOK WHAT THEY COULD CARRY AND HID.

WHEN THEY KNEW THE BOATS WEREN'T GOING TO LEAVE THEM BEHIND, THEY CAME OUT OF HIDING – FROM EVERYWHERE.

HARRIET MANAGED TO KEEP THEM CALM UNTIL THEY WERE SAFE.

HARRIET'S GROUP DESTROYED MOST OF THE CONFEDERATE SUPPLIES. THEY ALSO FREED OVER 750 SLAVES. NEARLY ALL THE MEN JOINED THE UNION ARMY.

THE SOUTH NEEDED SLAVES TO PROVIDE THE ARMY WITH SUPPLIES. THE MORE SLAVES THEY HAD, THE MORE WHITE MEN THERE WERE TO FIGHT INSTEAD OF HAVING TO FARM.

BUT A FREED SLAVE COULD ALSO FIGHT.

THE UNION WAS SCARED THAT IF THEY LET FREED SLAVES FIGHT, SOME UNION STATES WOULD SIDE WITH THE CONFEDERATES. BUT WITH THE WAR GOING BADLY, THE UNION NEEDED MEN. THE FIRST BLACK REGIMENTS WERE FORMED. AT FIRST, THE ARMY DIDN'T BELIEVE BLACK SOLDIERS COULD FIGHT. THEY WERE ONLY THOUGHT FIT FOR GUARD DUTY, LIKE BURYING THE DEAD. THEY DIDN'T EVEN HAVE UNIFORMS!

COLORED SOLDIERS WERE PAID LESS THAN WHITE. IT TOOK SOME TIME BEFORE THAT INJUSTICE WAS PUT RIGHT.

ARE THEY SOME OF THE COLORED TROOPS?

YES, THE 54TH MASSACHUSETTS, FORMED IN 1863.

THE 54TH WERE FREEMEN VOLUNTEERS.

BOUFF

THEIR COMMANDER WAS COLONEL ROBERT GOULD SHAW.

THE 54TH PROVED THEIR WORTH AT FORT WAGNER. HARRIET WAS ALSO THERE.

FORT WAGNER WAS A CONFEDERATE STRONGHOLD, WITH 1,700 WELL-ARMED SOLDIERS. IT WAS ON THE NORTHERN SHORE OF MORRIS ISLAND AND GUARDED THE SOUTHERN TOWN OF CHARLESTON, SOUTH CAROLINA. BEFORE CHARLESTON COULD BE CAPTURED, FORT WAGNER HAD TO *FALL*.

ON JULY 18, 1863, THE 54TH MASSACHUSETTS, LED BY COLONEL SHAW, MARCHED ALONG THE MUDFLATS AND DUNES OF MORRIS ISLAND. THEIR JOB WAS TO *TAKE* FORT WAGNER.

WHEN THE 54TH WERE A FEW HUNDRED YARDS FROM THE FORT, THE CONFEDERATE FORCES *OPENED FIRE*.

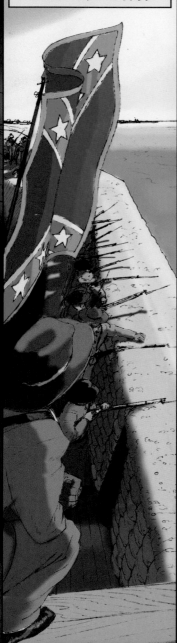

COLONEL SHAW WAS AMONG THE FIRST TO REACH THE TOP OF THE FORT'S WALL. HE CRIED 'ONWARDS BOYS!' AND FELL DOWN *DEAD*. A BULLET HAD HIT HIM IN THE HEART.

AFTER THE BATTLE, THE CONFEDERATES DUG A PIT TO BURY ALL THE DEAD BLACK SOLDIERS.

IT WAS NORMAL TO BURY THE OFFICERS APART FROM THE MEN. BUT COLONEL SHAW'S BODY WAS THROWN INTO THE HOLE WITH ALL THE OTHER BODIES. THE CONFEDERATES *HATED* WHITE OFFICERS OF BLACK TROOPS.

THE CONFEDERATES LATER OFFERED TO REBURY HIM. BUT HIS FAMILY SAID THEY WERE PROUD HE WAS WITH HIS LOYAL MEN.

THE 54TH WAS BEATEN. OF THE 600 WHO STARTED THE ATTACK, 256 LAY DEAD OR WOUNDED. BUT THEY SHOWED THAT BLACK SOLDIERS COULD FIGHT.

AFTER THE FIGHTING, HARRIET AND THE NURSES TREATED THE WOUNDED. A MONTH LATER, THE CONFEDERATES ABANDONED THE FORT AND THE UNION TOOK CONTROL.

THE WAR ENDED IN 1865. HARRIET WAS TRAVELING HOME. THE ARMY HAD GIVEN HER A HALF-FARE TICKET...

YOUR TICKET'S WRONG, OLD WOMAN. THIS IS ONLY A HALF FARE.

TICKETS! TICKETS, PLEASE!

IT'S ARMY ISSUE. I EARNED IT!

STOLE IT MORE LIKE! I DON'T LIKE YOU **COLORED PEOPLE** ON MY TRAIN. YOU WANT TO RIDE, YOU GO WHERE YOU BELONG – **THE SMOKING CAR!**

SHE WAS STRONGER THAN HE BARGAINED FOR!

SOMEONE GIVE ME A HAND HERE!

IT TOOK THREE OF THEM TO MOVE HER.

THE FALL BROKE HER ARM. HARRIET WAS INJURED MORE THAT DAY THAN IN FOUR YEARS OF WAR.

BEFORE THE WAR, HARRIET HAD BOUGHT A SEVEN-ACRE PIECE OF LAND IN AUBURN FROM WILLIAM SEWARD. HE WAS ABE LINCOLN'S SECRETARY OF STATE, AN ABOLITIONIST, AND HARRIET'S FRIEND.

HARRIET BUILT A SMALL WOODEN HOUSE. THEN SHE BROUGHT HER PARENTS TO LIVE WITH HER.

IN 1867, HARRIET HEARD THAT JOHN TUBMAN HAD BEEN KILLED. SHE HAD MET NELSON DAVIES DURING THE WAR. HE WAS A BLACK SOLDIER AND YOUNGER THAN HARRIET.

IN 1869, THEY GOT MARRIED AND SET UP A BRICKYARD AND SMALL FARM.

IN 1869, HARRIET MET SARAH BRADFORD AND TOLD HER ALL OF HER ADVENTURES. SARAH WROTE A BOOK, 'SCENES IN THE LIFE OF HARRIET TUBMAN.'

THE MONEY HARRIET RECEIVED FROM THE BOOK WAS VERY USEFUL. AS WELL AS HER PARENTS, HARRIET LOOKED AFTER POOR PEOPLE IN NEED. ONE WINTER, HARRIET HAD TO BURN THE PICKET FENCE FROM AROUND THE HOUSE TO KEEP EVERYONE WARM.

THEN IN 1884, HARRIET GOT ALL THE FIRE SHE NEEDED. HER HOUSE BURNED DOWN!

THEY BUILT A BETTER HOUSE MADE WITH BRICKS. HARRIET'S PARENTS HAD DIED BY THIS TIME, BUT THE PLACE WAS STILL FULL OF HOMELESS AND SICK FOLK. THEY ALL NEEDED TO BE CARED FOR.

IN 1886, A NEW EDITION OF SARAH BRADFORD'S BOOK WAS PRINTED, CALLED 'THE MOSES OF HER PEOPLE. AMAZING LIFE WORK OF HARRIET TUBMAN.' HARRIET MADE GOOD USE OF THE EXTRA MONEY.

BUT THEY WEREN'T ALL GOOD TIMES FOR HARRIET. HER HUSBAND, NELSON, HAD DIED IN 1888.

SINCE THE WAR, HARRIET HAD BEEN TRYING TO GET BACK PAY AND A PENSION FROM THE GOVERNMENT FOR HER WORK AS A NURSE AND SCOUT. THEY SAID THAT AS SHE WAS WORKING UNOFFICIALLY, HER CASE DID NOT COUNT. WHEN HER HUSBAND, A WAR VETERAN, DIED, SHE ASKED FOR A WAR WIDOW'S PENSION. IT TOOK THEM SEVEN YEARS TO PAY HER. SHE RECEIVED $8 A MONTH!

HMM. I THINK IT'S STOPPED RAINING. YOU CHILDREN RUN ALONG. LOOKS LIKE I'VE GOT ANOTHER GUEST ARRIVING.

IN 1896, SUSAN B. ANTHONY, AN ABOLITIONIST, SUFFRAGETTE, AND FRIEND OF HARRIET'S, VISITED HER IN AUBURN...

SUSAN! HOW ARE YOU?

FINE, HARRIET, HOW ARE YOU?

HARRIET HAD SUPPORTED THE SUFFRAGE MOVEMENT SINCE ITS BEGINNING. SOME PEOPLE THOUGHT SUFFRAGE SHOULD ONLY BE FOR WHITE PEOPLE. BUT HARRIET FELT THAT THE FREEDOM TO VOTE SHOULD BE FOR EVERYONE.

HARRIET WENT TO ROCHESTER AND WAS THE HIGHLIGHT OF THE CONVENTION. IN 1897, THE ARMY FINALLY AWARDED HER A PENSION FOR HER WORK. SHE WAS ALSO GIVEN A SILVER MEDAL BY QUEEN VICTORIA OF BRITAIN. HER DREAM OF BUILDING A HOME FOR THE ELDERLY CAME TRUE. IN 1908, THE JOHN BROWN HOME WAS OPENED. IN 1911, HARRIET WENT TO LIVE THERE. IN 1913, HARRIET PASSED AWAY.

THE END

FREEDOM!

In 1865, slavery was finally abolished in the United States with the passing of the 13th amendment to the U.S. Constitution. The slaves were free, but their lives hardly improved.

THE HARRIET TUBMAN HOME
In 1896, Harriet bought a plot of land next to her house in Auburn, New York. She built a home to care for poor, sick, and needy former slaves. Originally called The John Brown Home, it was renamed The Harriet Tubman Home.

SHARECROPPERS
Even though slavery had officially ended, life was still very hard for the former slaves. In the South, many freed slaves worked as sharecroppers for white landowners. In return for their labor, they were entitled to a share of the cotton crop. They were badly treated and lived in severe poverty.

VOTES FOR WOMEN
In the middle of the nineteenth century, a movement began in the United States, aimed at winning suffrage, or the right to vote, for women. One of its leaders was Susan B. Anthony. Harriet became active in the movement and was a popular speaker.

Supporters of the suffrage movement, or suffragettes, were arrested and imprisoned for demonstrating in public.

Rosa Parks was fined ten dollars. For a year after her trial, thousands of black people refused to travel by bus as a protest.

Martin Luther King made his "I have a dream" speech in front of hundreds of thousands of people at the Lincoln Memorial in Washington, D.C.

SEGREGATION

Despite the abolition of slavery, discrimination against black people continued in the South well into the twentieth century. According to strict segregation laws, black people were not allowed to eat in the same restaurants as white people, attend the same schools, or ride together on the buses. In 1955, a black woman, Rosa Parks, was arrested in Montgomery, Alabama. She had refused to give up her seat on a bus to a white passenger.

"I HAVE A DREAM"

The arrest of Rosa Parks marked the beginning of Martin Luther King's (1929–1968) involvement in the growing civil rights movement and of his struggle to bring about equal rights for all Americans. On August 28, 1963, King gave his famous speech in Washington, D.C. In it, he stated that his dream was for his children to live in a country where they were not judged by the color of their skin, but by their characters.

GLOSSARY

abolish To put an end to something officially, such as slavery.

abolitionist A person who worked to do away with slavery.

amendment A change that is made to a law or legal document.

barricade A barrier to prevent people from getting past a certain point.

confederacy A union of states, provinces, tribes, towns, or people with a common goal.

Confederate A supporter of the Confederacy, or the Confederate States of America, the group of Southern states that broke away from the Union in 1861.

contraband Goods that are brought illegally from one place to another.

convention A large gathering of people who have the same interests, such as a political meeting.

debtor Someone who owes money.

discrimination Prejudice or unfair behavior to others based on differences in race, gender, or age.

garrison A group of soldiers based in a town or military post.

gourd A fruit with a rounded shape like that of a squash or pumpkin.

illiterate Not able to read or write.

Mason-Dixon Line The boundary between Maryland and Pennsylvania during the Civil War. It divided the Northern and Southern states.

measles A disease that causes coughing, fever, and a rash.

ordeal A very difficult or painful experience.

overseer A person who watches over and directs workers.

pension An amount of money paid regularly to a retired worker.

plantation A large farm found in warm climates where crops such as cotton, tobacco, coffee, and tea are grown.

Quaker A member of the Society of Friends, a Christian group.

rebellion When people rise up against an authority, leader, or ruler.

regiment A unit, or group of soldiers, in a professional army.

sedative A drug that makes you quiet and calm.

segregation The act or practice of keeping people or groups apart.

sharecropper A tenant farmer who gives a share of the crops as rent to the landowner.

spiritual A type of religious song.

suffrage The right to vote.

suffragette A woman who fought for women to have the right to vote.

treason The crime of betraying your country.

Union The Northern states of the United States during the Civil War.

volunteer Someone who offers to do a job, usually without pay.

Yankee Buckra A term used by slaves that referred to white people living in the Northern states.

FOR MORE INFORMATION

ORGANIZATIONS

The Harriet Tubman Home
180 South Street
Auburn, NY 13201
(315) 252-2081
Web site: http://www.nyhistory.com/harriettubman/

Harriett Tubman Museum and Learning Center
424 Race Street, Box 1164
Cambridge, MD 21613
(410) 228-0401

Rokeby Museum
4334 Route 7
Ferrisburgh, VT 05456
(802) 877-3406
Web site: http://www.rokeby.org/

FOR FURTHER READING

Armstrong, Jennifer. *Steal Away.* New York: Scholastic, Inc., 1993.

Bisson, Terry. *Harriet Tubman: Antislavery Activist.* Broomall, PA: Chelsea House Publishers, 1991.

Kallen, Stuart A. *Life on the Underground Railroad.* Farmington Hills, MI: Gale Group, 2000.

Lilley, Stephen R. *Fighters Against American Slavery.* Farmington Hills, MI: Gale Group, 1998.

Sadlier, Rosemary. *Tubman: Harriet Tubman and the Underground Railroad.* Kent, WA: Pacific Pipeline, Inc., 1996.

Stein, R. Conrad. *John Brown's Raid on Harpers Ferry in American History.* Berkeley Heights, NJ: Enslow Publishers, Inc., 1999.

INDEX

A

abolitionists, 3, 5, 14–15, 18, 31, 41, 43
Africa, 6, 8–9
Andrews, John, 32
Anthony, Susan B., 3, 42–44

B

Bailey, Joe, 29
barricade, 23
Bowley, John and Kessiah, 16
Bradford, Sarah, 41–42
Brodess, Edward, 10, 12, 14
Brown, John, 3, 31, 34

C

Civil War, 3, 7, 32–40
confederacy, 7
Confederate, 7, 34–35, 38–39
contraband, 32–33
convention, 43

D

Davies, Nelson, 41–42
debtor, 12
discrimination, 45
Douglass, Frederick, 3, 28, 31

F

54th Massachusetts, 37–39
First South Carolina
        Volunteers, 33
Fort Sumter, 7, 32
Fort Wagner, 37–39
Fugitive Slave Act, 5, 18

G

Garrett, Thomas, 3, 23
Green, Harriet, 10

H

Harpers Ferry, 31
Hunter, General David, 33–34

I

illiterate, 22

K

King, Martin Luther, 45

M

Mason-Dixon Line, 15
Montgomery, Colonel James, 34

N

Nalle, Charles, 29–31
Niagara Falls, 29

O

overseer, 13

P

Parks, Rosa, 45
pension, 42–43

Q

Quakers, 3, 21, 23
Queen Victoria, 43

R

rebellion, 3
Ross, Ben, 10, 14, 19

S

Second South Carolina
        Volunteers, 34
sedative, 28
segregation, 45
Seward, William, 41
Shaw, Colonel Robert Gould, 37–39
slave catchers, 21, 23–24, 28
slave trade, 6, 8–9
spiritual, 17
St. Catharines, 18, 31
Stewart, John, 14

Still, William, 3, 18
suffrage movement, 3, 43–44

T

treason, 31
Tubman, Harriet
    awarded medal, 43
    becomes a conductor, 18
    becomes a nurse, 33
    becomes a scout and spy, 33
    birth of, 10
    death of, 43
    escapes to the North, 15
    gets involved in the suffrage movement, 43
    grandparents, 6, 8–9
    head injury, 13
    hides with pigs, 12
    marries John Tubman, 14
    marries Nelson Davies, 41
    opens a home, 43
    parents, 6, 10, 14, 19, 41–42
    settles in Auburn, 41
Tubman, John, 14–15, 17, 41

U

Underground Railroad, 3, 5, 18, 20–21
Union, 7, 32–37, 40

Y

Yankee Buckra, 36

Web Sites

Due to the changing nature of Internet links, the Rosen Publishing Group, Inc., has developed an online list of Web sites related to the subject of this book. This site is updated regularly. Please use this link to access the list:

http://www.rosenlinks.com/gnf/tubman

NF   7/05